Cliff Richard ▮ Chubby Checker ▮ Nat King Cole ▮ Shirley Bassey ▮ Dion ▮ Quincy Jones ▮ Alma Cogan ▮ Matt Monro ▮ Adam Faith ▮ The Beatles ▮ Duke Ellington ▮ The Beverley Sisters ▮ Helen Shapiro ▮ The Hollies ▮ Billy J. Kramer and the Dakotas ▮ Carl and the Cheetahs ▮ Julie Driscoll ▮ The Vernons Girls ▮ The Swinging Blue Jeans ▮ Brian Epstein ▮ George Martin ▮ Georgie Fame ▮ Cilla Black ▮ Jess Conrad ▮ The Animals ▮ Peter and Gordon ▮ Ella Fitzgerald ▮ The Dave Clark Five ▮ Mary Wells ▮ The Shadows ▮ The Yardbirds ▮ Eric Clapton ▮ The Supremes ▮ The Beach Boys ▮ Martha and the Vandellas ▮ The Miracles ▮ Marvin Gaye ▮ Gene Pitney ▮ Beau Brummel ▮ P.J.Proby ▮ Long John Baldry ▮ Graham Bond ▮ Smokey Robinson ▮ Stevie Wonder ▮ Gerry and the Pacemakers ▮ Peter Noone ▮ Elkie Brooks ▮ Burt Bacharach ▮ Brian Auger ▮ Astrud Gilberto ▮ Dizzy Gillespie ▮ Eartha Kitt ▮ Sonny and Cher ▮ David Bowie ▮ Rod Stewart ▮ Cilla Black ▮ Liza Minnelli ▮ Little Richard ▮ Lee Dorsey ▮ Pink Floyd ▮ Lulu ▮ The Pretty Things ▮ Joe Cocker ▮ Ron Wood ▮ Liberace ▮ Spencer Davis ▮ Barclay James Harvest ▮ Edgar Broughton ▮ Steppenwolf ▮ Deep Purple ▮ Syd Barrett ▮ Mama Cass ▮ Kevin Ayers ▮ Mike Oldfield ▮ Sweet ▮ CCS ▮ Marc Bolan ▮ Michael Jackson

THE END OF INNOCENCE

**Photographs from the decades
that defined pop: the 1950s to the 1970s**

Scalo Zurich — Berlin — New York

With thanks to David Hughes, Janie Orr, Janet Lord, John Mouzouros and
Kate Calloway of EMI Records, and to all the photographers

The End of Innocence
Edited by Liz Jobey
Production of the photographs: Original black and white photographs
were printed by John Mouzouros and Paul Jeffries under the supervision
of John Mouzouros, London
Design: Hans Werner Holzwarth, Berlin
Production: Steidl, Göttingen
© 1997 for the text: Gordon Burn, Liz Jobey
© 1997 Apple Corps Ltd for the photographs on pages 14, 95, 220 and 243
© 1997 EMI for the photographs except for the above
The painting *The Beatles,* 1963 – 1968, by Peter Blake,
is reproduced by courtesy of the artist / DACS
© 1997 for this edition: Scalo Zurich – Berlin – New York
Head Office: Weinbergstrasse 22a,
CH-8001 Zurich / Switzerland
phone 41 1 261 0910, fax 41 1 261 9262
Distributed in North America by
D.A.P., New York City;
in Europe and Asia by
Thames and Hudson, London;
in Germany, Austria
and Switzerland by Scalo.

First Scalo Edition 1997
ISBN 3-931141-47-0
Printed in Germany

Contents

The Supremes on the roof-terrace at EMI's Manchester Square offices, London, October 1964

Liz Jobey **Introduction**

Who could have known in the 1950s how great the cultural significance of pop music would be? Certainly the photographers who worked for EMI Records during the 1950s and early 1960s would have found it hard to imagine their pictures being pored over by cultural historians 40 years later. It's taken nearly that long for pop — essentially the music of the present — to develop a sense of its own past, largely because the generation responsible for pop, the post-war baby-boomers growing up in the late 1950s and 1960s, has enjoyed the most protracted teenagerdom of all time.

Those EMI photographers couldn't have known, either, which of the hundreds of groups and solo singers they photographed each year would become famous. Could they tell the difference between the one-hit wonders, global superstars and a bunch of no-hopers? It doesn't look like it: one of the joys of looking through these photographs is the way they reveal how indiscriminately the photographers treated the acts they were assigned. Who knew what lay in store for Tony Rivers and the Castaways or the Beatles when, within months of each other in 1963, they were taken up on the balcony of EMI's Manchester Square building, told to look down into the camera and smile? Only now do we know which became the most famous pop group of all time and which ended up among Sir Cliff Richard's regular backing vocalists.

EMI moved into their new building in Manchester Square — a landmark in pop-people's London for the next 30 years — in 1960. It wasn't until 1965, however, that they set up a photographic department responsible for organising photographic sessions and producing the black and white publicity stills which, as well as being sent to record stores, the national press, and group fanzines such as *Beatles Monthly,* supplied EMI's own pop magazine, the *Record Mail* (the classical music division had *Record Times*), which ran features about all its new "popular" groups. The 2^1/$_4$ inch-square format of the photographs was no accident: it matched all three record-sleeve formats (7-inch 10-inch and 12-inch), and fitted the column widths of the in-house magazines. Janet Lord, who is still responsible for their photo archive today, was moved from EMI promotions to set up this new photo department, and one of her first jobs was to sort through a pile of old negatives and contact sheets from early popular music artists, identify them and set up a filing system. They included not just what we recognise today as pop musicians, but early MOR crooners such as Nat King Cole and Matt Monro, comedians and light entertainers, such as Peter Sellers and Ken Dodd, and long-forgotten female soloists who had once shared a season at Blackpool or Great Yarmouth with Tommy Steele, or Helen Shapiro, or the Beverley Sisters. Identifying the pictures could be difficult: sometimes only the name of the act was scribbled on the envelope containing the negative, sometimes — surprisingly rarely —

the date or — equally rarely — the name of the photographer. Though the identity of some of the photographers, such as John Dove, who took early photographs of the Beatles, is recorded, many remain anonymous. Staff photographers were in the habit of marking only the first session of the year — 6.1.63 for example — and then not recording any further dates until the start of the following year. By 1965 some groups had changed labels, or already disappeared, or changed their image so as to be almost unrecognisable (there are several sessions marked "do not use: new image"). Even now, some pictures have never been accurately dated, and are marked VH, Very Historic. Among them is an impossibly young-looking Cliff Richard, circa 1959 (when he would have been 18 or 19) with the pianist Russ Conway (in heavy eye make-up); and a clean-cut dark-haired young man in a suit, white shirt, collar and tie, called Paul Raven, who, 20 years later, would reappear bedecked like a human Christmas tree as Gary Glitter.

The setting up of a photographic department was a response to the pop revolution that took place in the three years between the Very Historic pictures and the release of the Beatles, first album, *Please, Please Me,* in 1963 — a year that even then began with the Black and White Minstrels at the top of the album charts. Until the end of the 1950s, film soundtracks had dominated the LP charts. Early pop vocalists such as Elvis and Cliff Richard stuck to singles and EPs. Cliff released his first two albums on Columbia/EMI in 1959, the year after Elvis's first two, but neither of them could topple the best-selling LP of 1959 — the soundtrack to the film-musical *South Pacific,* which stayed at number one for the entire 52 weeks of the year. By the end of 1963, the Beatles' second album was only deposed by the Rolling Stones in an album-chart duet that would endure for the next three years.

Parlophone and Columbia, the two EMI pop labels, competed with with Decca, Philips and Pye to snap up new talent as fast as it arrived off trains from Liverpool or Sheffield or Newcastle. By 1965, the archive is full of pictures of the four- or five-piece, all-male, identical-ly-dressed groups that dominated EMI's British recording roster: the Beatles, the Hollies, Billy J. Kramer and the Dakotas, Gerry and the Pacemakers, the Animals, the Swinging Blue Jeans, Manfred Mann, Freddie and the Dreamers … happy, smiley, clean-looking young men who all seem to be having a wonderful time in front of the camera. In those days photographers complied with a house rule that said a group should be photographed *as a group,* and no one member should be singled out. It was later, in response to fan-demand, that individuals were celebrated by their own pin-up portraits.

For many of the groups photographed in the early and mid-1960s, their contract-signing at Manchester Square and the subsequent recording at the Abbey Road studios would have been their first trip to the capital. A euphoric post-signing leap down the steps of one building or the other became a photographic standard. Some groups were less ebullient. "I remember the Animals in particular," Janet Lord said. "They were a motley lot — I don't mean that in a snobbish way — but they were. They just sat around the office, and none of us could under-stand a word they said, and it turned out they were only interested in where they could get proper beer. They were strangers in London, simple as that."

A day in the life of the photo department consisted of a request from the promotions and publicity people for a photographer to set up a session with a group. If it was a new signing, these photographs, which arrived with the new single, would be the first time journalists, record shops and customers could see who they were listening to. Locations depended on available time, the requirements of the group's management, which might want a tie-in with the current release, and the ingenuity of the photographer. Studio shots, through they do exist, were un-popular, as group members resented the intrusion of a photographer into a recording session — though these often made the most natural-looking pictures. As the pace hotted up, however, ingenuity seems to have been in short supply. Manchester Square and its close environs supplied the backdrops for hundreds of photographic sessions — the roof, the famous balcony (which is now ritually cemented into the restaurant balcony of EMI's new building in West London), the spiral staircase, the parking meter, the Rolls Royce, the railings and the main entrance, all take on a talismanic quality as they reappear, increasingly familiar and un-changing, behind a parade of new faces, fashions, and attitudes that shift radically as the decade moves on.

If the current record was an inspiration, it was often taken literally — the Animals outside the Rising Sun pub (for their single "The House of the Rising Sun"); or the Dakotas mocking-up a magic carpet ride on the floor of the Manchester Square foyer (for their "Magic Carpet" single). Unfettered by political correctness, it seems to have been accepted photographic practice to rope in a pretty girl to enliven the expressions of a particularly wooden group as she sauntered past. And as late as 1966, in what must have been a last fling before both musicians and photographers became more sophisticated, Lee Dorsey was photographed at a London depart-ment store which sold children's toy ponies-on-wheels to illustrate his hit "Ride Your Pony". He went along with it happily, judging from the pictures, and took the country singer Bobby Goldsboro with him for company.

What marks out these photographs from the early years of pop is the good-humoured compliance with which so many acts greeted the corniest suggestions for a picture. Who could imagine the Supremes being taken straight off the plane and up onto the roof of Manchester Square, presented with a rolled black umbrella each, and asked to adopt various music-hall dance-routine poses, without the bowler hats, but presumably in homage to their arrival in the City of London? Would you dress up in a dappled suit and get down on all fours in the park, even if you did belong to a group called the Cheetahs? Would you clamber up a tree in your new polka-dot two-piece, like Lulu, or don a bikini and heels and squeeze into a Mini like Fay Fisher? Of course not. But perhaps their naivety was just a measure of how limited a life-expectancy most pop acts assumed theirs would be. The contrast between these cheery, willing faces and the moody attitudinising of today's stars is as great as the difference between the pipe-smoking, besuited staff photographers who took the early pictures, and today's superstar-photographers, whose behaviour and salaries match, and in some cases exceed the self-importance and earning power of the people they photograph. All this because image has become the crucial marketing tool, and an entire service industry has developed around pop stars, not just of managers and personal publicists, but of stylists and designers and image consultants and personal trainers and hair and make-up artists and soothsayers and stock-brokers, all of whom are involved in the way their client is packaged and promoted, crucially, by television and video rather than by still photographs and record sleeves.

In 1965, however, it was Radio Luxembourg, rather than television, which was the chief purveyor of pop music to the general public. Its shows were sponsored by record companies and each week EMI showcased artists from both Britain and America in what was called first the Monday, then the Friday Spectacular, recorded in the tiny reception studios at Manchester Square after which the audio tape was sent to Luxembourg's London office to be transmitted the following week. The week's acts would be interviewed by resident DJs and give a short rendition of their latest record in front of an invited audience. Captives in that tiny space, this presented the perfect photo-opportunity for a "live" publicity shot, and the signature ruched satin curtain that comprised the weekly Spectacular set unifies photographs of acts as far apart as the Swinging Blue Jeans and Stevie Wonder. Looking at them now it seems impossible that such proximity to major stars could be sustained in the face of growing fan-mania, Indeed, by the time P. J. Proby came on the show, the rope barrier was totally useless, and the fans were obviously far more strenuous than the old commissionaires had bargained for.

As the second half of the decade wore on, live performances became more important for the publicity of a particular act. Freelance photographers and even amateur enthusiasts had always supplemented the staff photographers at EMI, who were increasingly required to do an early session in the morning and stay out to cover a live performance much later the same night. The growth of pop music was breeding a new bunch of photographers who found the music scene lucrative enough to specialise in. This increase in freelance photographers coincided with the realisation on the managements' part of how important image could be in the potential success of a group, and they wanted to have more say in its control. Increasingly groups negotiated the right to use a freelance photographer of their own choice, and the record companies, keen to keep their major recording stars, complied. By becoming successful, a group claimed the right to participate in its own promotion strategy — and strategy is what it was. Pop was becoming a hugely competitive international business. Naivety was giving way to cynicism, as a new breed of marketing executive, skilled in manipulating both the media and the consumer, lectured their clients in the seriousness of their commitment. No wonder groups forgot to smile for the camera.

Changes in photographic practices paralleled those taking place in photographic requirements. Live concerts required smaller cameras and faster film: 35mm replaced the $2\frac{1}{4}$ portrait format. There was more demand for colour, though black and white has never been completely phased out. The introduction of wide-angle lenses and the fashion for high-contrast prints with deep shadows only emphasised the growing self-awareness, the sullen poses taken up by groups on the verge of hippydom. The pictures no longer took their lead from the current single or album. Syd Barrett, the beautiful, troubled leader of the Pink Floyd, looks to have been almost hurt by the camera in the photographs that must have accompanied the release of his solo album in 1970 — entitled *The Madcap Laughs.* Long-haired hippy groups from America dressed in afghan coats, velvet, satin and beads, look barely conscious as they slouch together for what, on some contact sheets, are only two or three frames. This wasn't a new economy, it was a new attitude, and it meant that groups rarely turned up on time, alert or ready to co-operate: sometimes photographers were lucky to get them all together in more than a single frame before one left, or another was too stoned to carry on.

By the end of the 1960s, a new generation of photographers had taken over at EMI. Long-haired and leather-jacketed, they looked more like the groups they were photographing, and used 35mm film and natural light which gave their pictures a reportage-style quality that was completely different from the formal, detailed portraits produced by the Rolleiflexes and Hasselblads. Live concert work was becoming the norm, but some favourite photo themes remained. Even the Sex Pistols were photographed signing their EMI contracts in 1976 in exactly the same way that the Pink Floyd had been photographed signing theirs almost ten years before (after which the Floyd obligingly leapt down the steps in glee).

In the years since the end of the 1960s, the shift towards freelance photographers, live performance pictures, colour, and image-control has continued. Photography itself discovered a new-found self-importance during the 1970s, which only increased claims for artistic licence, and made the photographer's role in image-management more crucial. Eventually, at EMI, the staff photographers were disbanded. The 1988 copyright act secured ownership of the negative for the photographer, rather than the commissioning agent, and the days of photo-approval and limited prints have placed "artistic control" firmly in the hands of the photographers.

In 1995, EMI moved again to new headquarters in West London. The upheaval, and the consciousness that their centenary year was coming up, prompted John Mouzouros, who heads the photographic darkroom in West London, to print up some of the old negatives out of curiosity. Artless, done on the hoof in many cases, corny and old-fashioned, nevertheless a treasury of photographs was contained in those thousands of slim brown envelopes, a piece of history waiting to be acknowledged. Now Janet Lord is set up in a new building at Hayes, outside London, where once again she is cataloguing and cross-checking and shaking her head in wonder as at least two new generations of fans exclaim over her photographs and listen with fascination to her stories. For her and her small group of photographers, it was just a job. Occasionally she might offer a word of encouragement, or a cup of tea, to a nervous new performer, but for the most part she was dedicated to keeping the files in order. And what would have been there now, if she hadn't?

Liz Jobey is a writer and editor in London.

14   Dezo Hoffmann's photograph of the Beatles being photographed on the steps of Abbey Road Studios, London, February 1963

Gordon Burn **The End of Innocence**

In November 1963, at the beginning of the week that would end with President Kennedy being assassinated in Dallas, an American journalist called Michael Braun caught up with the Beatles on the first full-out Beatlemania tour of Britain. The Beatles had just racked up their third successive number-one with "I Want To Hold Your Hand", and Lennon, McCartney, Harrison and Starr had suddenly become the most instantly recognizable people in the country. ("YEAH! YEAH! YEAH! You have to be a real sour square not to love the nutty, noisy, happy, hand-some Beatles" began the *Daily Mirror*'s band-wagonning editorial for 5th November 1963, cele-brating the Beatles' epochal appearance the previous evening at the Royal Command Variety performance — the one where Lennon asked the commoners to clap and the people in the richer seats to rattle their fucking jewellery [expletive, when it came to it, reluctantly deleted].)

The craziness was just getting underway, but Braun met the Beatles in peculiarly low-key (possibly carefully stage-managed) surroundings. They had played two shows at a hall in York and were in their hotel bedrooms finishing their dinners. A table filled with the dirty dinner dishes was at the foot of Ringo's bed. Ringo was sitting up in bed dressed in pyjamas. Paul was padding round the room, also in pyjamas. John wandered in wearing a T-shirt and an old pair of trousers. George had fallen asleep after eating in the room down the corridor that he was sharing with John.

Probably because he was an American, and America was the territory that the Beatles were then concentrating all their energies on breaking (they would occupy all five top places on the *Billboard* charts within months of the interview taking place), they seemed to have been generous with their time, polite, smart, scabrous within bounds, charming and funny as always — at once remote and accessible, glamorous and homely, anxious to give value. From a distance of nearly 35 years, though, it is what is going on in the background of Braun's piece that constantly trips the eye and telescopes time and most completely evokes the period.

There's a wireless standing on Paul's bedside table in the British Rail hotel and it is obviously tuned to the BBC Light Programme. The old standard "Our Love Is Here To Stay" is the first song that comes out of it, followed by "Old Devil Moon". "That was 'That Old Devil Moon' in a magnificent interpretation by the MacGuire Sisters," says the radio. "Now, straight from the moon to the stars." The radio plays "Swinging on a Star". Next up is "You'll Always Be Mine" by the fading teen-dream (fading fast, like all the milk-slop crooners and Max-Factored warblers since the emergence of the Beatles), Mark Wynter.

("What the normal pop artist does is, he learns to tap dance," Lennon tells Braun at one point. "We don't want to learn to dance or take elocution lessons.") Ringo snaps the radio off when he thinks because John is talking he isn't listening. John gets him to turn it back on again. "And now, a number from Xavier Cugat…"

Pyjamas, carpet-slippers, laddish jokes, steam radio, a sense of self-deprecation and moderation bred into them during their childhoods in Liverpool (Paul picks up the phone to order drinks from room-service: "Six single Scotches," he says. And then, remembering that they are the toppermost of the poppermost: "No. Make that doubles.").

Albert Goldman, in common with most Beatle biographers, saws away at how Beatles tours were a six-to-a-bed, eight-in-a-night daisychain bacchanalia. If that was true later in their careers (how much later — two hours, three?) there is not a hint of it here. The scene that Braun describes is in many ways a re-enactment of scenes that would have been taking place in many British living-rooms and chintzy front parlours on a winter's night in 1963.

In 1963, things in England were not so very different than they had been in the 1950s, even the 1940s, when announcers on the BBC had been required to wear evening jackets, and engineers at Electric and Musical Industries — EMI — Britain's biggest and therefore most establishment-minded record company, wore long white coats like boffinated B-movie scientists, and even jazz drummers were not allowed to remove their jackets during recording sessions, as if EMI were a masonic institution, some kind of gentlemen's club, with committees and rules and regulations and a door policy — which in many respects, of course, it was.

"The Duke of Edinburgh" is what the Beatles and EMI's other NEMS signings called their producer, George Martin (ex-Fleet Air Arm, ex-BBC), behind his back. Martin had joined EMI in 1950 as assistant to Oscar Preuss, head of A&R at Parlophone, known derisively within the company as the "junk" label because of a roster that included Sidney Torch and his Orchestra, Bob and Alf Pearson, and Roberto Inglez, "the Latin-American Scot".

Brian Epstein, manager not only of the Beatles but also Gerry and the Pacemakers, Cilla Black, Billy J. Kramer and the Dakotas, and the dozen or so acts that allowed EMI to out-earn the competition many times over through the 1960s, was similarly old-school. (NEMS — North End Music Stores — his management company, grew out of the family firm.) He'd got the ultra-mumsy "songstress", Anne Shelton, to perform the opening ceremony at the first NEMS record shop in Liverpool, for example; and it was the manager who encouraged the Beatles to pad out their set with mouldy old ballads like "Over The Rainbow" and "Besame Mucho", and "novelty" numbers such as "The Sheik Of Araby" when they went into the studio to make their first demonstration tape. Most notoriously (and it is this that history seems to be judging him on — see Albert Goldman and others on that spoilt rich-kid/the emasculating hand of Brian Epstein) he took the Beatles out of their grimy T-shirts and steamy leathers and put them into the shiny mohair mercurochrome suits, part-band balladeer, part-bank clerk, which had been standard showbiz issue in Britain since the "American Invasion" of the immediate post-war years.

"Offend nobody". For three decades, from the Thirties to the Fifties, this had been the aesthetic that informed the BBC's understanding of its listeners' leisure needs. Output, according to an early Corporation memorandum, must attempt "to blend the maximum of wholesome brightness with the atmosphere of quiet leisure about the hearth". The "radio hearth" featured heavily in the advertising of all wireless manufacturers. Even in the early Sixties, pop programming in Britain was mainly confined to programmes such as "Children's Favourites" and "Two-Way Family Favourites" and "Housewives' Choice", presented by DJs who put themselves over as either house-master or matron.

The British record industry was, equally, run by men and women with little experience of or interest in popular culture or popular taste. As the cultural critic Simon Frith has written: "They, too, began with the assumption that popular music was worthless — it was its worth-lessness that made it commercially exploitable." Pop singing was regarded as an apprentice-ship for becoming an all-round family entertainer; a "sincere" performer in the great showbiz tradition. Pop records had to be cheerful and uplifting, they had to appeal across the board.

The publicity and promotion industries — the smiling professions — were in their infancy in those days. This was before the fashion for violent and unflattering lighting; before fish-eye lenses and unnatural angles came in. The smudgers touched out wrinkles, spots, heat rashes without waiting to be asked. Because a pop star shown with a drink or a cigarette could risk jeopardising his (or, more likely, her) career, drinks and cigarettes were routinely air-brushed out. The lensmen themselves wore Tootal scarves and trilbies; carried rolled umbrellas. At the beginning, they used flash-guns that exploded and left an acrid, sulphurous after-smell.

"It was a very clean and tidy age," one of the first British pop photographers, Harry Hammond, has said. "There was no such thing as a rebellious entertainer. If you were an entertainer you were expected to look well-groomed — editors liked to see the artist nicely presented."

For the men, this meant cleft chins, crinkly hair, boxy shoulders and trousers with zero crotch-definition — the conventional notions of beefcake. Women, on the other hand, were exaggeratedly feminine, with up-thrust busts and hand-span waists and generally a lot of padding, pleating, stiffening, corseting and boning going on. Shirley Bassey embellished this with a "difficult" reputation and a classic rags-to-riches story. The Beverley Sisters did it in triplicate, and the "giggle girl" Alma Cogan with a laugh in her voice. Nina's (of Nina and Frederick) special gloss was a Grace Kelly headscarf and lashings of aristocratic *hauteur*: She, it was rumoured, was a real-life countess (or maybe it was that he was a real-life count), so full marks for taking the indignity of exposure to seaside kitsch with such good humour, and accepting a dressing-room with mildew lifting the flocking from the walls, its fizzing lights and clanking pipes, with such exemplary élan! The camera never lies.

EMI, in common with its main rival, Decca, didn't begin to take on good art directors and designers until the late Sixties. Until then anything out of the ordinary was often dismissed as "arty". If they wanted to develop an image in order to sell themselves, it was up to the artists and their managers to hire the services of a photographer. In their early days the Beatles used a freelancer called Dezo Hoffmann. It was Hoffmann who snapped them leaping into the air and performing "camerabatics" in Margate on the South Coast (later recreated for the film poster advertising *A Hard Day's Night*, and by the members of Manfred Mann in this collection). These bits of business in the "monkey shots", as the groups involved invariably referred to them, served the same purpose as the fast cutting and visual excess in today's pop videos: it was an attempt to suggest a sense of spontaneity and energy in a situation where none actually existed; it gives the impression of the lights being on when, in fact, there's really nobody home. In video clips it has the added effect of disguising the inferior quality of the sound reproduction of most televisions, making the music sound louder.

It was in their choice of Dezo Hoffmann's replacement, though, that the Beatles revealed a sophisticated grasp of the changes exposed so graphically in the pictures from the EMI archive: the transformation of the record industry into the rock business, and of the Beatles themselves from "happy little rockers" to a trillion-grossing entity, in the space of only two or three years.

The British photographer Robert Freeman was a friend of Lawrence Alloway, the man credited with coining the term "Pop art". Through Alloway, Freeman also had connections in the Fifties with the London Independents' Group, an innovative collection of artists, architects and writers whose aim, broadly stated, was to use popular culture to cut high-brow culture down to size. (Interestingly, the Independents included Frank Cordell, a musical director for EMI, who talked about pop music and Stockhausen in the same terms). Freeman had encountered Robert Frank, together with several Beat writers, in New York in 1959, and Frank's raw, frequently out-of-focus, "unfinished" photographs influenced the photographs Freeman started to take on his return to London, first of artists in their studios, then the new generation of pop musicians.

When he encountered the Beatles for the first time, in August 1963, to shoot the stark, flat portraits that would end up being the cover of their second album, *With The Beatles,* Robert Freeman had recently completed a film about the young British Pop artist, Richard Smith. (Freeman went on to be the stills photographer and credits designer for Dick Lester on the films *A Hard Day's Night*, in 1964, and *Help!*, in 1965. "We work much harder with someone like Robert Freeman or [the British fashion photographer Norman] Parkinson than with the nationals, who only want a cheesy grin," McCartney told Michael Braun. And it is clear that pictures of the Beatles and others taken by Freeman, like pictures of the Rolling Stones taken by their friend Michael Cooper, are much closer to self-portraiture than the publicity shots squeezed off during photo-calls at Abbey Road Studios or at the EMI building in Manchester Square. There is a powerful subtext to these pictures and it is this: that it is the company that is in control; the power is still with them, although, towards the end of this book — the Yardbirds, Pink Floyd — it is possible to sense it ebbing away as star-power begins to assert itself.)

Richard Smith's obsessions were the worlds of advertising and packaging, of brand emblems and corporate logos: "the universe of commodities". He had made vast paintings based on the corporate symbols for Chase Manhattan Bank, Revlon, and the American radio station WADO, but by 1962 – 63 looming, polychromatic cigarette packs were turning

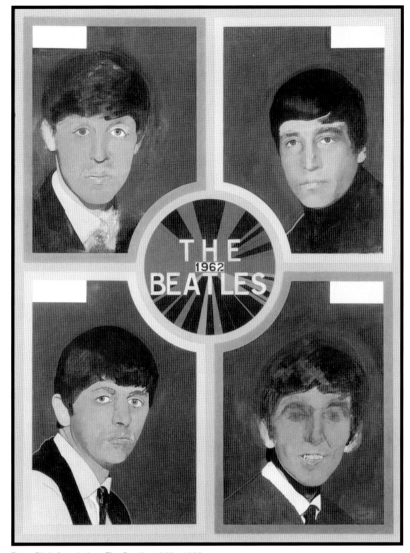

Peter Blake's painting, *The Beatles* 1963 — 1968

out to be the subjects of his best work. Smith's big idea was that single images, although beginning as casual, banal, or anonymous may, through reproduction and repetition, come to assume a talismanic or iconic significance. It is a conclusion Andy Warhol had come to at roughly the same time, though via a different route, with his celebrity portraits and commodity paintings.

The passage of the Beatles from Mop Tops to fetish objects and consumer icons was marked as early as 1963 by the painter Peter Blake, and by another British artist, Pauline Boty, who included images of them, along with Cassius Clay, JFK, Elvis, the bullfighter El Cordobes, and Lenin, in her painting "It's A Man's World 1". In the Blake painting, the Beatles have already become logofied, singled out as symbols of their era: their individual features are smeared and scumbled; they are identifiable as "Beatles" by their ties, their jackets, their ironising attitude and, most of all of course, by their most prominent branding feature, their hair. The fact that Blake's painting was based on a publicity picture of the kind collected here (assembled in the form of a quartered-off souvenir postcard) is a commentary on the fact that these pictures were usually intended to have a secondary life on posters, programmes and cheap flyers; as images transferred to mugs, lamps, pennants and other merchandise —always out there somewhere, circulating, multiplying, reproducing like spores in the world. Warhol liked to work from similar, unauthored, "dumb" or debased material.

It seems reasonable to suppose, given his background and his friendships with artists such as Richard Hamilton and Richard Smith, that Robert Freeman, on hand to photograph the Beatles on almost a daily basis during their most formative period, should be credited with making at least some contribution towards the focusing and streamlining of their image. It is impossible to know how big a part he actually played in the promotional fashioning of the Beatles (he is mentioned only in passing or as a footnote in all the best-known Beatles books). But from the pictures in this collection we can see the way some of the other groups on EMI tried to create trademark looks for themselves. There's the four members of the Four Sights with their four pairs of Buddy Holly / Hank Marvin / John Lennon glasses. There's Carl and the Cheetahs with their synthetic fur boots and synthetic fur suits, and the fake foppishness of Beau Brummel and the Noble Men. By 1964 at the latest, though, the "English" look — bum-freezer jackets, stove-pipe trousers, Chelsea boots, nylon "knitted" ties, tab collars, a look rugged and curiously feminised at the same time — has become generic. The Swinging Blue Jeans, the Mojos, the Searchers, the Merseybeats, the Undertakers, Gerry, Herman, Billy J. are as little different from each other as the rows of squeegeed images in a Warhol repeater painting, or the multiple portraits of gas stations and parking lots, their landscape so banal and familiar, made by the West Coast artist Ed Ruscha at about the same time.

The androgyny was quite a departure from the macho swagger and straight-up-and-down maleness that had been typical of an earlier generation of recording artists (and it was still more or less typical of the members of the great Tamla Motown groups who came over from the US to Britain throughout the Sixties). Up until about 1967, though, and in spite of the youthquake fashions and brattish attitudinising, everybody — performers, photographers, record company "suits" — was recognisably part of a shared culture. Everything was still *heimelig* — homely. It was after 1967 that a sense of the *unheimlich* — the unhomely, the uncanny, started to creep in; a sense of something new, foreign and hostile invading the old, familiar, customary world. The something new, of course, was psycho-pharmaceutical, and it accounts for the hairies and out-there-o-nauts and zomboid exquisites who start to slouch into the frame and stare wall-eyed into the camera.

The hairiness, the beads and the buckskin jackets, the new who-the, what-the, doing-my-head-in-man, stoned address to camera, were all meant to represent a rejection of the hype and gimmickry and plain fraudulence of the monkey shots and all the straight old, bad old ways of The Industry. There was a rejection of commercialism and "selling out". "Crucial to the argument was the suggestion that stars and fans were somehow in alliance against the business that actually mediated between them," writes the critic Mary Harron. "Financial dealings, record company strategy, marketing and publicity campaigns were rarely mentioned; these were irrelevancies, or, at worst, a corruption of the true spirit of rock'n'roll." Once rock stars were morons; now they were oracles. The surprising thing was how quickly and easily the new hippydom fitted into the existing commercial structure. The counterculture became just another teenage pop fad, another pitch. It would take the punks, in the mid-Seventies, to rediscover the virtues of old-fashioned pop-hype: the publicity stunts, the image-making, the fan magazines, the very artificiality seemed more honest than rock's heavy sincerity.

"People have this obsession," Mick Jagger said once, many years ago, when he was merely pushing 40. "They want you to be like you were in 1969. They want you to, because otherwise their youth goes with you, you know. It's very selfish, but it's understandable."

One of the most poignant programmes on British radio is "Sounds of the Sixties". Presented by Brian Matthew, it goes out on Saturday mornings in almost exactly the spot that Matthew ("This is your old mate Brian Matthew saying, 'That's all for this week — *seeeeeeeee-ya* next week.'") held throughout the beat boom years. As well as the old hits, there are "SOS" features for obscure B-sides and album tracks and appeals for information about Robbie of the Untamed or Allan, Shane Fenton's drummer, or Terrys and Julies found and lost at the Tottenham Royal or the Newcastle Majestic on twangy evenings more than thirty years ago. Record requests are played for ruby weddings and sixtieth birthdays, and many references are made to spreading waistlines and thinning hair and why can't I have some of what Cliff's on.

At the time of their taking, the pictures in this book aspired to being nothing more than ephemera — cheap throwaway ten-by-eights; things to be attached to hand-outs on the off-chance that they might make a one-or two-column filler in the pages of the *Record Mirror* or *Melody Maker* or *New Musical Express*. But that was in a time before the media *became* our community; before we were a people of, by, and for the image, when it was still believed that some images were so fugitive that they couldn't be grabbed, retrieved or replayed. "The environment of the image *is* the landscape," as the American academic Frank Lentricchia has put it. "It is what (for us) "landscape" has become, and it can't be switched off."

Here are images that feel both nostalgic and impersonal — bright, confused, innocent, blurred, with a dated, hopeful glow around the edges.

Gordon Burn is the author of two novels, *Alma Cogan* (1991), which won a Whitbread Award, and *Fullalove* (1995). His biography of the Yorkshire Ripper, Peter Sutcliffe, *Somebody's Husband, Somebody's Son,* won an Edgar Allen Poe Award in the United States. He wrote the text for the artist Damien Hirst's book, *I Want to Spend The Rest Of My Life Everywhere With Everyone One to One Always Forever Now,* and is currently working on a book about the Frederick West murders in Gloucester, England, and a novel. He lives in London.

Photographs from the decades that defined pop

Cliff Richard and Russ Conway, c 1959   **25**

Chubby Checker demonstrates the Twist, c 1961

Chubby Checker demonstrates the Twist, c 1961

Paul Raven (later Gary Glitter), c1961

Cliff Richard's 21st birthday party, October 1961

Mike Sarne and Wendy Richards, c 1962

Gary "US" Bonds arriving at London Airport, 1962

Johnny Burnette arriving at London Airport, April 1962

Johnny Burnette, Gary "US" Bonds, and Gene McDaniels, April 1962 **41**

Peter Gordeno in the EMI recording studio, 1962

Muriel Squires in the EMI recording studio, 1962   **43**

Carol Deene promoting her new single, 1962

Shane Fenton (later Alvin Stardust) giving a radio interview, 1962

Blackpool Tower, the summer season, 1962

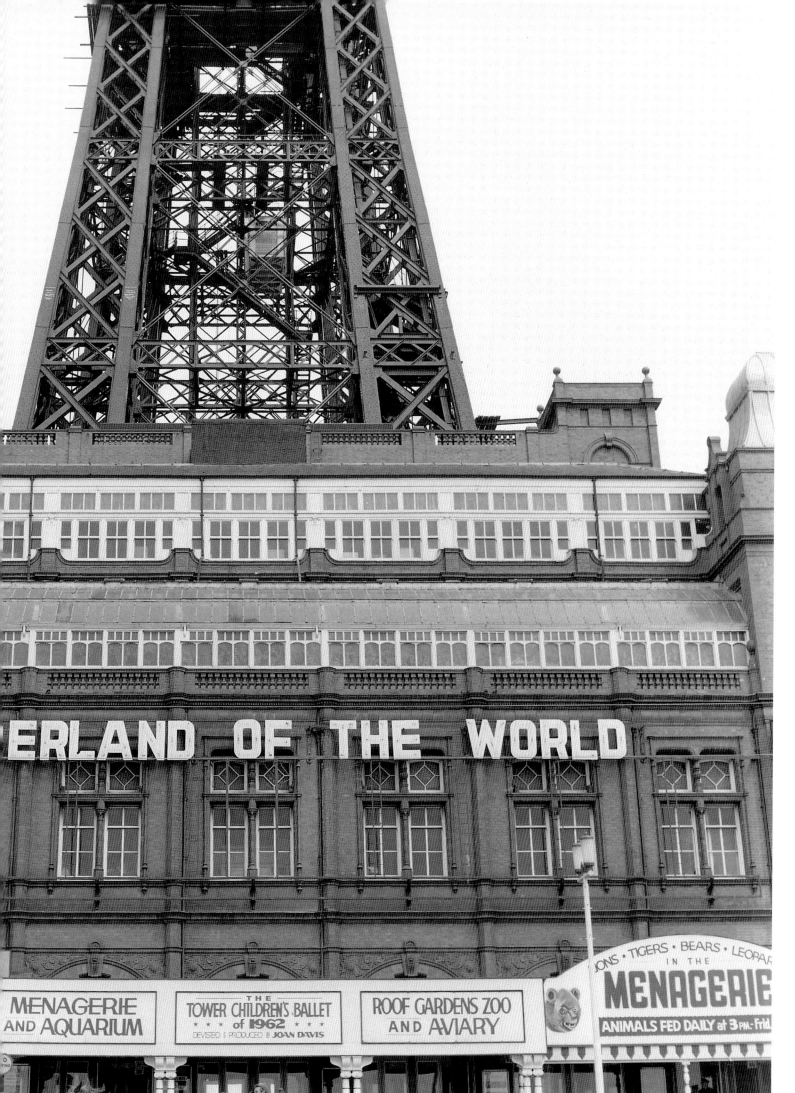

ERLAND OF THE WORLD

MENAGERIE
AND AQUARIUM

THE
TOWER CHILDREN'S BALLET
of 1962
DEVISED & PRODUCED by JOAN DAVIS

ROOF GARDENS ZOO
AND AVIARY

IONS · TIGERS · BEARS · LEOPAR
IN THE
MENAGERIE
ANIMALS FED DAILY at 3 PM. Frid.

Nina and Frederick, Blackpool, 1962

Ken Dodd, Blackpool, 1962

Nina and Frederick backstage, Blackpool, 1962

Dion at the Friday Spectacular, 1962

Frank Ifield, 1962

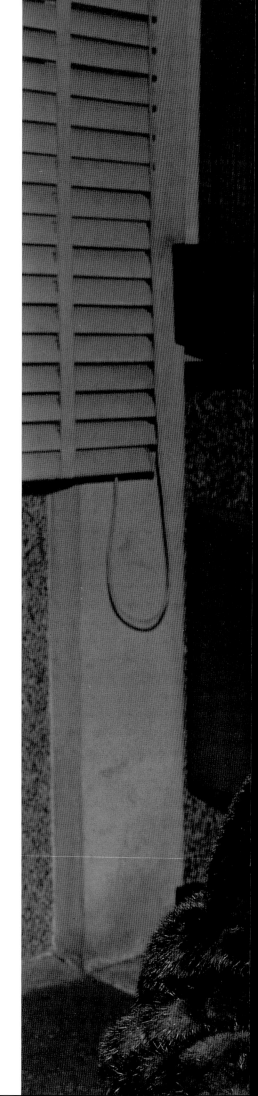

Joe Loss and his Band, Hammersmith Palais, London, 1962

Nina and Frederick in the recording studio, November 1962

Adam Faith, 1962

Carol Deene at Shepperton Studios recording "It's All Happening", 1962

The Beatles' first recording session, "Love Me Do", October 1962

The Beatles with George Martin, seated right, at Abbey Road Studios, February 1963

Johnny Hodges with a member of the Duke Ellington Orchestra, 1963

Duke Ellington, at the piano, and his Orchestra in the TV studio, 1963

The Beverley Sisters, Great Yarmouth summer season, 1963

HMV record store, Oxford Street, London, 1963

THE NEW WAY
TO BETTER HEARING

Shane Fenton and Eden Kane, March 1963

Helen Shapiro at the 150th Friday Spectacular, 1963

The Hollies at the 150th Friday Spectacular, 1963

The Four Sights, 1963

84   The Dakotas promoting their "Magic Carpet" single, Manchester Square, 1963

Madeline Bell, 1963

Tony Rivers and the Castaways, 1963

Brian Epstein with the Beatles' first album, April 1963

The Beatles, "Please Please Me" album cover session, Manchester Square, March 1963

Shirley Bassey in the recording studio with George Martin, 1963

Georgie Fame, Christmas 1963   **99**

Host Shaw Taylor with fans at the Christmas Spectacular, 1963

BILLY J. KRAMER
with THE DAKOTAS

Listen...

mono

The HMV shop, Oxford Street, London, 1964

Cilla Black, 1964

Jess Conrad, 1964

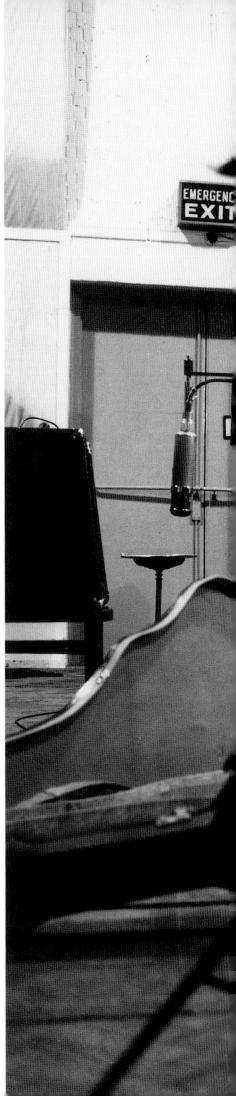

Peter and Gordon in the recording studio, April 1964

Ella Fitzgerald in the recording studio, April 1964

The Dave Clark Five, Birmingham, April 1964

The Shadows, April 1964   **117**

118   The Paramounts (later Procol Harum), 1964

The Yardbirds, with Eric Clapton, second left, May 1964

The Animals, after releasing "The House of the Rising Sun", June 1964

The Supremes' first British tour, October 1964

The Supremes with Sir Joseph Lockwood, chairman of EMI, October 1964

Taking a photo-call on the roof of Manchester Square, 1964

The Supremes' Christmas portrait, November 1964

The Beach Boys arriving at London Airport, October 1964

The Miracles with Smokey Robinson and his wife, Claudette, 1964   (Overleaf) performing on Ready, Steady, Go!

Marvin Gaye, 1964

Mary Wells, 1964

Cliff Richard, 1964   **139**

Freddie and the Dreamers, 1964

The Noble Men, Beau Brummel's backing group, 1964

Beau Brummel, 1964

Cliff preparing to play Aladdin in "Aladdin and his Wonderful Lamp", Christmas 1964

The Seekers, Piccadilly Circus, February 1965

The Graham Bond Organisation, from left, Ginger Baker, Jack Bruce, Graham Bond, Dick Heckstall-Smith, February 1965

The Bo Street Runners, 1965 **169**

Burt Bacharach, at the piano, with the Manfred Mann group, June 1965

Brian Auger, July 1965   **173**

Eartha Kitt during a recording session, April 1965

Sonny and Cher, August 1965

Davy Jones (David Bowie), August 1965

186 Davy Jones and the Lower Third, August 1965

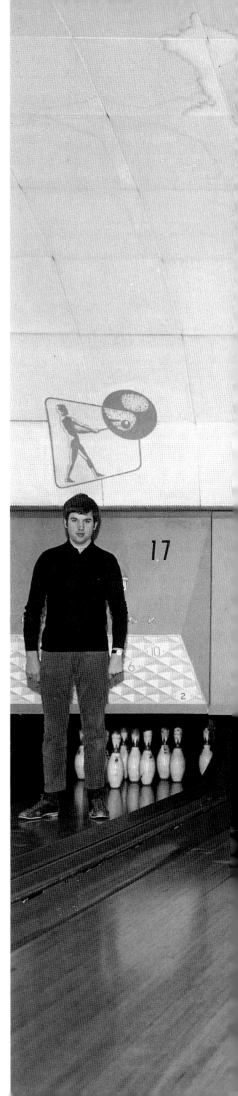

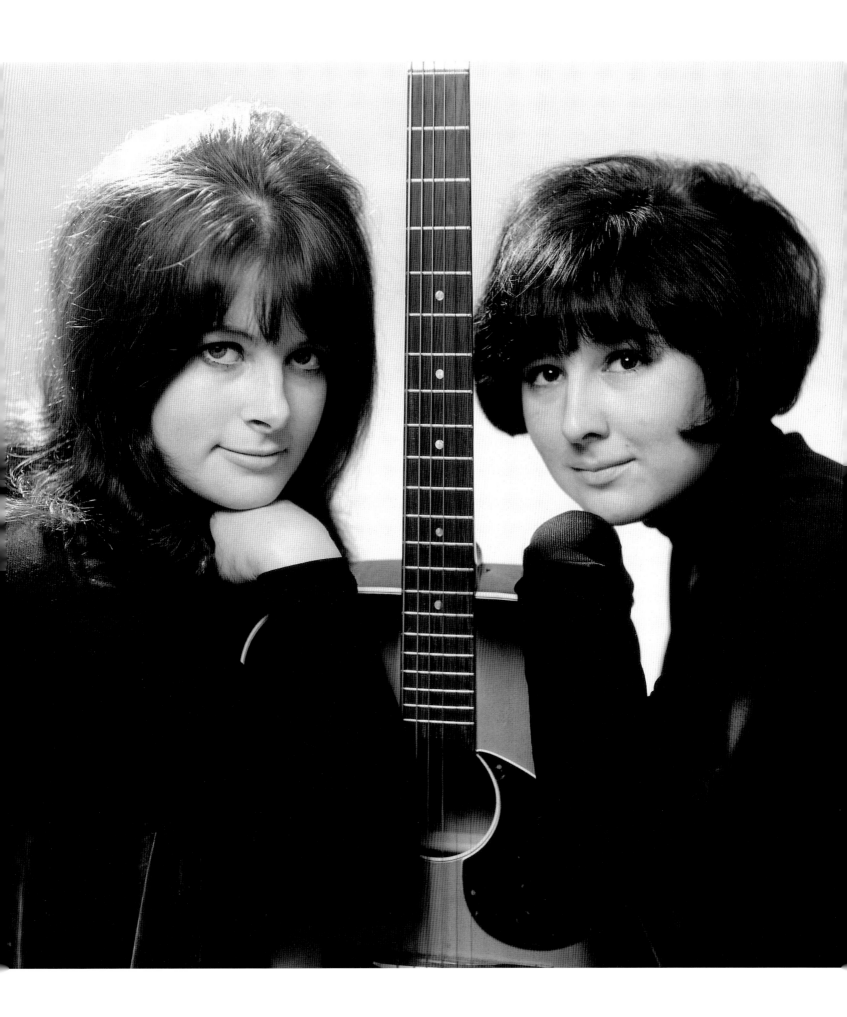

Twiggy and Ann, December 1965   **193**

195

Cilla Black, April 1966   **197**

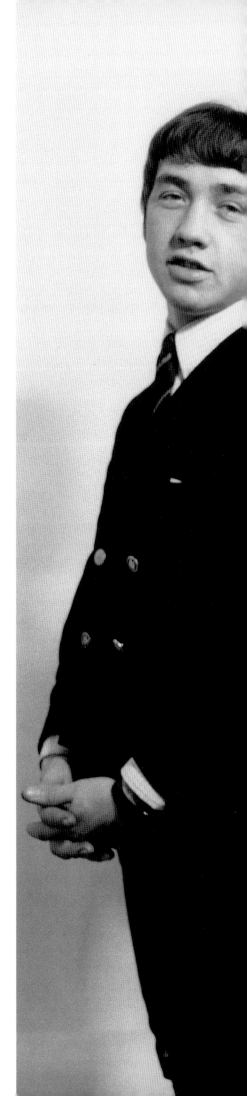

Derek Lee skateboarding, June 1966

Rod Stewart with Shotgun Express, October 1966

The 'N'Betweens (later Slade), November 1966

→ Name

First Name

Address

City

State

ZIP

Country

Phone

Fax

○ **I would like to receive** regular information about the Scalo list. Please put me on your mailing list.

Additional remarks

SCALO

Place Stamp

→ **Scalo**

Mailing address for

■ **Europe and Asia**

Weinbergstrasse 22a

CH-8001 Zurich / Switzerland

■ **USA**

155 Avenue of the Americas

New York, N.Y. 10013

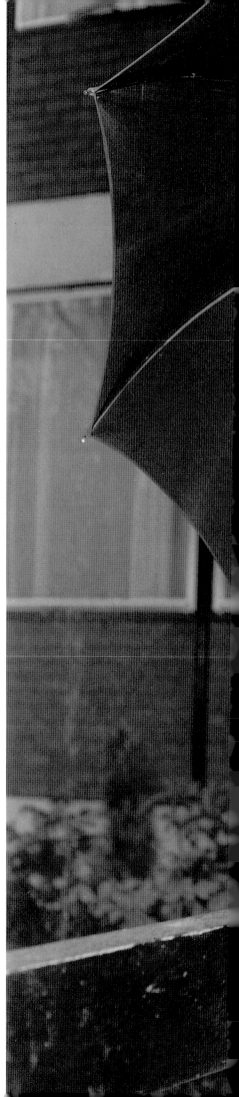

Inez and Charlie Foxx, January 1967

Disc-jockey Simon Dee amid psychedelia, April 1967

Pink Floyd signing their contract, February 1967

Pink Floyd, March 1967

The Beatles recording "Sergeant Pepper's Lonely Hearts Club Band", 1967

The Jeff Beck Group, from left, Ron Wood, Jeff Beck, Mickey Waller, Rod Stewart, November 1967

Liberace arriving on his "Grand Tour" at London Airport, April 1968

Barclay James Harvest, March 1968

Paul and Tim, November 1968

238   Pink Floyd, with David Gilmour, centre, May 1968

The Edgar Broughton Band, the Roundhouse, London, May 1969   (Overleaf) Three Dog Night, May 1969, and The Beatles' last photo session, 22 August 1969   **241**

Deep Purple, September 1969   **245**

Mama Cass, October 1969   **249**

Kevin Ayers, right, and Whole World, March 1970

Mike Oldfield, January 1970 **251**

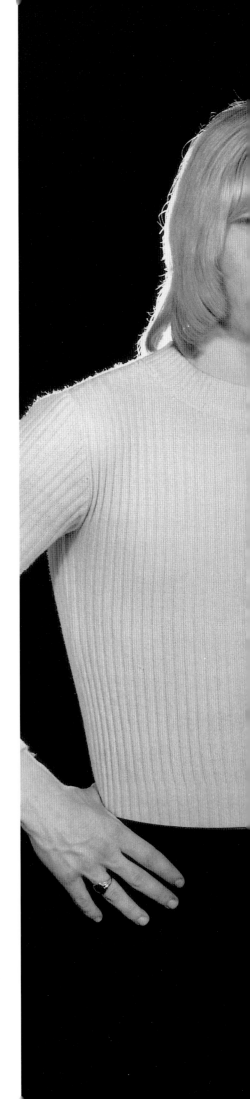

Alexis Korner, with CCS, October 1970

Marc Bolan visiting the EMI factory, Hayes, June 1972

Marc Bolan signing autographs, Hayes, June 1972

257

Michael Jackson, on tour with the Jackson Five, November 1972

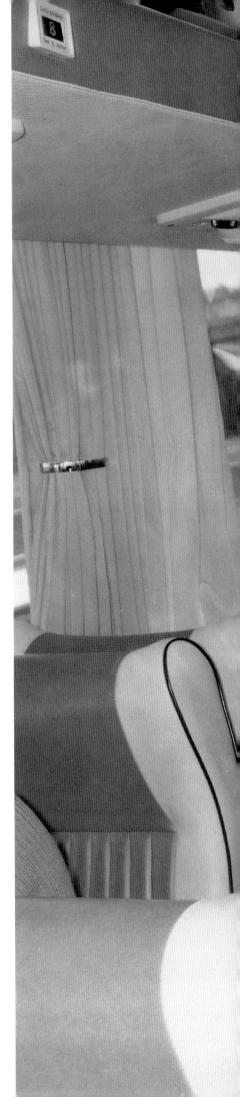

Album covers

1970

1960 →

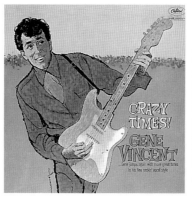

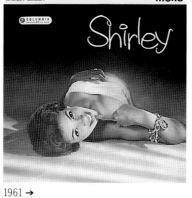

1960 →

1961 →

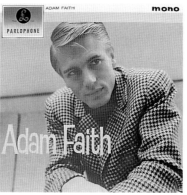

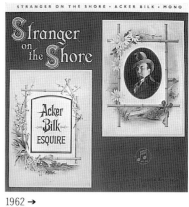

1961 →

1962 →

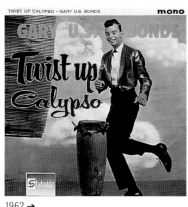

1962 →

1962 →
1963 →

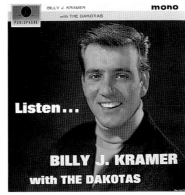

1963 →

1964 →

1964 →
1965 →

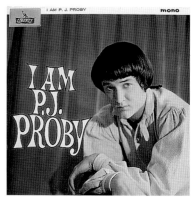

1965 →

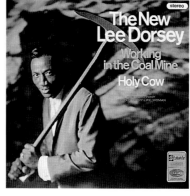

1965 →

1966 →

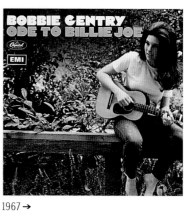

1966 →

1967 →

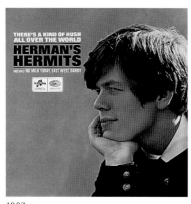

1967 →

1967 →   1968 →

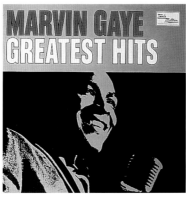

1968 →   1969 →

1969 →   1970 →

1970 →

Cliff Richard ▮ Chubby Checker ▮ Nat King Cole ▮ Shirley Bassey ▮ Dion ▮ Quincy Jones ▮ Alma Cogan ▮ Matt Monro ▮ Adam Faith ▮ The Beatles ▮ Duke Ellington ▮ The Beverley Sisters ▮ Helen Shapiro ▮ The Hollies ▮ Billy J. Kramer and the Dakotas ▮ Carl and the Cheetahs ▮ Julie Driscoll ▮ The Vernons Girls ▮ The Swinging Blue Jeans ▮ Brian Epstein ▮ George Martin ▮ Georgie Fame ▮ Cilla Black ▮ Jess Conrad ▮ The Animals ▮ Peter and Gordon ▮ Ella Fitzgerald ▮ The Dave Clark Five ▮ Mary Wells ▮ The Shadows ▮ The Yardbirds ▮ Eric Clapton ▮ The Supremes ▮ The Beach Boys ▮ Martha and the Vandellas ▮ The Miracles ▮ Marvin Gaye ▮ Gene Pitney ▮ Beau Brummel ▮ P. J. Proby ▮ Long John Baldry ▮ Graham Bond ▮ Smokey Robinson ▮ Stevie Wonder ▮ Gerry and the Pacemakers ▮ Peter Noone ▮ Elkie Brooks ▮ Burt Bacharach ▮ Brian Auger ▮ Astrud Gilberto ▮ Dizzy Gillespie ▮ Eartha Kitt ▮ Sonny and Cher ▮ David Bowie ▮ Rod Stewart ▮ Cilla Black ▮ Liza Minnelli ▮ Little Richard ▮ Lee Dorsey ▮ Pink Floyd ▮ Lulu ▮ The Pretty Things ▮ Joe Cocker ▮ Ron Wood ▮ Liberace ▮ Spencer Davis ▮ Barclay James Harvest ▮ Edgar Broughton ▮ Steppenwolf ▮ Deep Purple ▮ Syd Barrett ▮ Mama Cass ▮ Kevin Ayers ▮ Mike Oldfield ▮ Sweet ▮ CCS ▮ Marc Bolan ▮ Michael Jackson